The Red Hour

The Red Hour

POEMS BY

ROBIN BEHN

HarperPerennial
A Division of HarperCollinsPublishers

HarperCollins books may be purchased for educational, business, or sales promotional use. For information please write to Special Markets Department, HarperCollins Publishers, Inc., 10 East 53rd Street, New York, NY 10022.

FIRST EDITION

Designed by Jessica Shatan

Library of Congress Cataloging-in-Publication Data
Behn, Robin.
    The red hour / Robin Behn.
    p.   cm.
    ISBN 0-06-096952-0 (pbk.)
    I. Title.
PS3552.E412R4   1993   92-56262
811'.54—dc20

93 94 95 96 97 ❖/HC 10 9 8 7 6 5 4 3 2 1

Acknowledgments

Some of these poems first appeared in the following publications, to which grateful acknowledgment is made:

Agni Review: "The Name of God"; *The American Voice:* "Five O'Clock in Your Childhood," "Those Unitarian Sundays"; *Crazyhorse:* "The One Girl on the Soccer Team," "30 Windsor"; *Denver Quarterly:* "Slow Movement in G"; *Field:* "Grackles," "On Giving My Father a Book About Roses"; *Indiana Review:* "Ten Years After Your Deliberate Drowning," "Vision Near Ice"; *Iowa Review:* "The Bassoonist," "Etiquette," "Five O'Clock," "French Horn," "Windy Popples, Late October," "Husbandry," "Midwestern," "The Saving Grace of Mozart"; *Missouri Review:* "Aubade"; *New England Review:* "The Oboist" (winner of the NER narrative poetry competition); *The Ohio Review:* "The House in the Clearing"; *Ploughshares:* "The God Hole"; *Poets for Life: 76 Poets Respond to AIDS* (Crown, 1989): "Maybe the Jay"; *Seneca Review:* "The Year He Tried Business"; *Spoon River Quarterly:* "The Pit."

"Midwestern" was also collected in *Best American Poetry 1992* (Scribner's, 1992).

"French Horn" was also collected in *The Pushcart Prize* XVIII.

It is a pleasure to thank the National Endowment for the Arts, the Alabama State Council on the Arts, and the University of Alabama for grant support that made this writing possible; Yaddo, the MacDowell Colony, the Ragdale Foundation, the Djerassi Foundation, the Getty Center for the History of Art and the Humanities, and the Virginia Center for the Creative Arts for time and space; and Sheila Gillooly.

For Patti

The spirit moves, but not always upward.

—THEODORE ROETHKE

Contents

I

Ten Years After Your Deliberate Drowning   3

The One Girl on the Soccer Team   5

Those Unitarian Sundays   6

The Oboist   8

The Summons   10

The Bassoonist   12

30 Windsor   15

Five O'Clock in Your Childhood   17

First Flame   20

Sleeping in the Shrine Room   23

At the Symphony   25

The God Hole   27

II

Our Mutual Friend in Heaven   31

Etiquette   33

The Saving Grace of Mozart   35

Grackles   37

On Giving My Father a Book About Roses   39

Windy Popples, Late October   42

Late Valentine   43

Slow Movement in G   45

Storm Bulletin   47

Aubade   49

Midwestern   51

Christmas at the Buddhists'   52

French Horn   54

III

Vision Near Ice   59

The Name of God   61

Maybe the Jay   63

Husbandry   66

The Sousaphonist   70

The Pit   71

The Year He Tried Business   77

The House in the Clearing   79

Five O'Clock   81

The Red Hour

I

Ten Years After Your Deliberate Drowning

Since then, I work at night.
   Against the glass the identical moths

open themselves to me. The lamp
   illumines the decorative eyes

evolution has granted them.
   So don't think I'm alone.

To them I am *the* light.
   Days I don't come with flowers,

please think of these white petals
   pressed into this pane.

Pale shapely trapezoids—
   they too remember your shoulders.

If I don't light the light
   for x nights in a row . . .

Tell me what x is.
   You must be in x by now.

Sometimes one travels several inches
   on its thready legs—

an old idea alighting
   on a new ledge in the brain.

I used to think—what thing was it
   that I had failed to do?

Now I just see your body,
   filled almost up with water,

harden in my arms, then break
   —so much does it desire to be filled—

against the real river for good.
   The eyes through which I see this

are impervious to light.
   This I have learned from the moths:

open your wings when you must
   and flash the inner eyes

of a creature so big it could eat
   both you and the thought that would eat you.

Most of what follows I see:
   how there are more and more,

how they never fly away.
   Nor do they rest in pairs.

Whatever made these wings
   is remaking yours now

somewhere in the workshop where the thing is extracted
   that leaves behind the dark.

Out there their clustered shadows
   spill darker kissmarks on that dark.

The One Girl on the Soccer Team

Luck opened that day the way a tree drops its leaves—
not to any *me* or *you* but to something
seasonal: fall
soccer, or the headaches that began that fall
—dishes I threw at some wall in my head,
at the pictures the children's books had hung there—,
or the ball, a saucer gone sci-fi, 3-D suddenly,
landing square against my head.
In my neck's green stalk I felt
the shudder and the rightness of the
gap where the one head
had been kicked off by this other, flying head,
and then the others stood above me, closing the gap
where the smell of grass leaked through.
They were pinnied like racehorses, they
suddenly knew my name and the brave ones
spoke and spoke it—
but even that was not enough to make me happy that fall.
How can it be enough to have one's mind knocked back
into the larger, grassy mind
and have the angel appear: she had me
under her antiseptic wing, it was
the soft school nurse, it was
the bed I've always dreamed of,
the screened-off domesticity
where some human voice keeps asking how you are
and then begins a lovely story.

Those Unitarian Sundays

First they took the "hell" out—
a committee had ordained it—
and then the son-of-god part, and then,
by degrees, the "He."

What was left in the learned hymns
we pressed against the backseat window
like Totfinder stickers that mark
where children dream their catastrophic dreams

was my sister's voice, tenor,
and my own seemingly-descant second alto
and the thing that had no name
that made us sing as our drunk father

made the car sing, dipping, expressive,
to the breakdown lanes' ledger lines and back
to the sudden counterpoint of headlights
not our own.

We sang. We'd been taught to. We sang
the laundered songs whose *hell*, homeless,
huffed its red exhaust into my father's face
haloed by the steering wheel, we sang

and sang until *the Father* was forgotten,
till in our minds the car rose
one angelic inch above the pavement,
hydroplaning on the bridge, while

Lovely secret gardens grow, we sang,
Underneath the sea
—what was it they advised, do you
let the car fill almost up and *then* pry the doors, or

wait like a whole-note sealed on the bottom,
singing *lovely, lovely* as the medics' "jaws of life"
lift you to the cadence of marveling sirens
rolling their red eyes till the

miracle quiets them: everyone
alive and, look, two girls
still singing as the car ascends
into the rest of the air!

—The way, those Sundays, *his* red eyes
would finally roll, heaven-touched, into the rearview
where they found us and his deep voice found
its way to *Lovely, girls.*

The Oboist

That year the oboist practically lived
at our house, fingering the pearl keys
    of my sister's blouse, making
a white note of her that squeezed
    through the lips of the double doors called "French"
like the kisses we imagined and adored.

And we adored how he arrived:
fresh from his lesson, stepping seriously
    off the bus to the airbrakes' sighs,
launching himself at us like a wobbly sail
    as if, at his back, he still felt the two winds
from the four half-lips of his birthparents mouthing

their reedy, reedy goodbye *goodbyes*
from a place tinged with ether where everyone else,
    dressed in white, dressed him
in white and set him out, crisp,
    into the arms of a new someone, out
and out, as he'd continue to set out,

a big boy now with his afternoon luggage,
his two neat black satchels—the oboe
    in one and in the other
the knives with which one learns
    to carve a place to put
the song—.

My sister
was a someone, and a song and
    where he carved—we could see it

in the ligature of her thin smile
   all ready for his slurring as he came up the walk
and through the mouth of the old house,

   depositing his small derby
in the center of the table
   and ascending, *vivace,*
at her hefty side the curved stair
   to the room we'd have to scrub stars
off the ceiling of later, ceiling their twin-cries

   curved into a regal arch
over the dot of the hat, the whole house
   gathering around that fermata of wishes
some conductor kept
   holding, holding as if the end
were too stubborn to come.

The Summons
HAWAII, 1977

When the wind finished cleaning
the air around his head
D. saw blues branch to violet where
its face—it *had* a face—was
a separate thing from sky, though, no, he
couldn't quite describe its head
zooming in to form a helmet of blue ice
around *his* head the minute he looked—

It hurt to look, he said,
the thing wouldn't appear again but still it
tried to help as if it knew about those TV ads
for frozen headache pillows—
it was like wearing the sky for a head.

But that it should appear to *him*
—interloper, tourist—
seemed to add to his belief
(we came to call it his "belief"
though he had never mentioned
wanting-to-believe).

Now we will never know
whether we would have seen
a small man cradling his head
at the base of the large mountain
or whether we would have grown cold and left.

As they were taking him
off of the ancient island
(a grown man, but his actual mother
had had to be summoned to coax him,
shuffling his new Thorazine shuffle,
up the gangplank onto the plane)
he saw that the planet was furrowed
(and we said, yes, it *is* furrowed,
astronauts see that, too),

but beyond the obvious worry, he said,
he could not see what else it was god thought,
except there was a bluishness
separate from, *worse* than
the other wrinkled blues.

They must have banked.
He said bright wings obscured
whatever was left of the view.

The Bassoonist

His was a life that ached for form early on
It needed something outside
    to rhyme with what it was
something it could leave behind later

And so he played bassoon
because bassoon, like life, was hard
    No one, hardly, played it
So he was in great demand

The sound it made (we knew this)
was really just his body
    honking against the twilight
it already belonged to

—a winged thing getting
not quite off the ground
    calling to the others
to *wait*

The face the double reed disappeared into
was pocked   well   cratered   really
    For its red and purple hues
there is no word but *angry*

He read the notes   barely
through a curtain of stringy hair
    But our quintet couldn't be
a quintet without him

which gave to his life
a certain necessity   lasting
        through a very long series of rehearsals
made even longer because his   ideas about

        rhythm were rather original
and he had to be convinced
        by the band director singing right into his ear
how his part went

        I don't remember now
how I first found out that his ugliness
        was guaranteed
to kill him before he turned thirty

        Thirty today, that field of volcanoes
then the knubby lips then the
        chewed straw of the double reed
appear to me again

        The face is still that pool
a small boy has fired fistfuls of pebbles into
        —He is that boy
That pond is his own face

        What self can do to itself
scares me   still
        But now I also wonder why a shame so deep
it burrows inward through the face

        and sucks at you from underneath
for the brief time forever is
        fell to this boy
to be our first example of

When the band took to the field
in our neat red blazers
        we felt him among us, out of step
like a bad cell

        A bassoon is too delicate isn't it
to march with in the rain
        So for a pretty price all of us
cut him off and didn't miss him

        Not when we reshuffled into a quartet
and couldn't find music
        for just
flute   clarinet   oboe   horn

        Not when we saw him propped in the bleachers
gazing on our formations with a scrambled contempt
        Not even when we saw the returned bassoon
dismembered   snug in its velvet casket

30 Windsor

For a while I lived alone above
the old lady, not talking
to her and not not
talking either—little *hello*'s over what
came into and out of our lives—
the mail and the garbage
of our lonelinesses.
Hers, I remember, she carried out back
one morsel at a time.
I'd come upon her opening
the lid of the smaller can
to deposit the tea bag and orange rind
from the breakfast her body
at that moment was still
mulling over like morning news.
What arrived
could be subscribed to:
Penney's catalogues, *Watchtowers*.
I'd peer down and see her removing
from the doorknob—studied surgical procedure—
the wads and wads of coupons for pizza.
No pizza ever came.
Though *someone* must have,
to take her on holiday those weeks the papers
collected on the walk like sticks desiring
a boy to rub them together,
and someone must have known why not
the cheery gurgle of sitcom but rather
a hot silence rose from the grate I stood on,
the wind from the furnace so strong
it billowed my nightgown into a sail

the whole house could ride away on,
so hot on my bare feet that if
I could stand it it might
start a fire and we both might
get rescued from the same nameable thing.

Five O'Clock in Your Childhood

The 5 o'clock pulls out. Hands on the tracks,
   you can feel the trainful
of mourners for your father
   shimmy westward.

Behind it, like the runners
   of a sled dropped at the door,
the tracks are warm a little while, then cold,
   then no one comes.

As it moves into the future,
   the train grows smaller.
Like hope, you think.
   It's hard to decide if the tracks

in front of you—over which
   ride the bodies of a few
scant relatives, over which
   rides the parched, pressed body of your father,

branded in the eyes
   of the bodies of scant relatives—
if those tracks you must stare
   into the death of the sun to see

are your future, or everyone's.
   Both choices are adult.
But there you are, thinking them.
   Already the train has dwindled

to the gray, squarish hat
　of a man who's walked the plank of the horizon.
Now the hat burns up, too.
　See? Little smoke feather.

Certain children on the platform
　aren't crying loud enough to hear.
This makes them invisible.
　And all of them are you.

Of course it's almost Christmas. The children
　who are both Christian and not fatherless stand singing
in flocks like the clumps of feathers
　you would gather in your fists.

When the train arrives
　it will probably leave
smokey bruises on the ceiling of the station.
　Indecipherable bruises

like the ones your mother gives you
　now that he has gone.
Maybe the hollowed-out angel that ate your father
　has iron-plated skin and a one-way visor

only God can see through
　so he's safe from your mother now.
And you? And you?
　Why go back to her house,

why leave these rails and their endless
　strip of earth—
good stretcher all the boys in the world
　might be rescued on.

But look. It's a real sled.
    Runners, not rails.
Nothing to do now but sail by yourself,
    belly-down, face-first, down

through the deep cut in the trees
    that looks like a man was shaving too fast
getting ready to die,
    even if it means you could crack up alone out there

like the last boy on earth
    who's survived age ten.
Somewhere near the bottom
    is the house you were born in.

First Flame

There we are again. X crutches up the walk
with the special heave assigned
to the miraculously saved
and rings the bell that releases me
into the sound of his arms.

Nothing about this is easy.
That he can't hold crutches plus a door,
that 20 years later he'll write me
from the permanent Outward Bound job
he finally holds down, that I will hate
the distant peaks he's paid to inch
the tough, rich boys up.

Right now we are trying to fix this in advance.
We are seeing a double-oh-seven
which is a movie, or some big number
of dates we've not yet had.

Right now he plays trumpet, perfect:
first chair, high Maynard-Ferguson-C's.
Right now he has beautiful, frightening lips
the light from the screen turns blue
as if they craved more blood, and hot jazz
is the only way he knows how to get some,
except now, here he is with a girl

who would be me.
Whole minutes transpire.
We segue to the world.
The crutches, parked, lean over the davenport

like awkward, delicate cranes over a promising oil field.
The oily breath of the anonymous investor they answer to
greases their bowed spines.

Naturally they expect lightning.
They wear their rubbery shoes.
They know how we require them since

the wind's big trumpet
blasted dear, mere Eagle Scout X
off the shoal from which he snorkeled
and slammed him against the lighthouse,
the goddamned *symbol* of warning:

above his shattered limbs
the light nodded *See? See?*
on the stem of its silver neck.

But the other scout, his friend,
held X's pretty, bloody face
pretty much out of the water,
clung to the rocks for them both,
and beat the all-afternoon ocean back
and flagged the passing chopper
and got them on national news.

In the photo ("recent") of X,
a fleck leads the other flecks
way up a steep white face
that carbon-dates pre-trumpet, -crutch.
The altitude looks Shangri-La,
or Oz, Nirvana, Nod . . .

His note says *some* boy (italics mine)
caught with a girl was grounded,
left behind, and took the shot.

Oh fleshy, punished kid,
is it better than what you and I want,
their billygoat try at ascension?

Sleeping in the Shrine Room

Like the princess, I can't sleep.
    Not a pea, but two knee marks
like sealed eyespots of the unborn
    stare up from the prostration board
beneath this cotton mat.

Blessed, these are the eyes to whom
    inner light is just what is—
not an idea yet,
    certainly not this thunk
of cartilage that fractures sleep,

the lingering sound of my sister's
    hazy body hurled through me as she
tallies up her assigned prostrations,
    almost and almost
falling out of her body.

On the wall,
    an 8 × 10 glossy of the Buddha's
current emissary,
    cheeky in the nightlight
of his gold satin robes.

Who are you, Undone Father
    whose baldness shines
like the inside of a body
    to illumine the merely
technically alive?

The year my sister met you
        she slept every night
in the lotus position,
        knees eroding, legs locked
to all but you . . .

In my dreams she will be
        that lotus flower, opening,
as incense sticks, planted like cattails
        in the altar's twin rice bowls,
enlighten the air.

At the Symphony

The organ's silver tubes store light
for later, to revive us, as
on cue, some lever's lowered and
the houselight stars go dim.
The chairs are bolted forward.
Like jockeys we hunker down.

Then slow, slanting rain
anoints us in the form
of bowstring horsehair stretched and drawn
again, again.

The tailless horse's shoulders
lumber under black sleeves.
Trumpets flair their nostrils,
trombones pump shiny, rain-wet legs,
cymbals, poised, gawk sideways at
the air, hoof-punctured, riddled with attempts,
then, oh, I *hear* you crash over—or back through—
the fence that keeps the dead composers dead,
removed from this "live" hall.

On its bulbous knee,
the English horn decrees
we'll exit *allegro* somehow
and leads us to a cadence,

a clearing where among
sunny, stable fifths we check:
All instruments unbloodied.
All human animals intact.

A rest between the movements—we bridle
at quiet. And cough
as though tightening chin straps,
and settle heads back onto stalks.

I have season tickets.
$59.00 this year.

This is how I try to bring you back
from where you dove in toward god.
I know that this is wrong. I know
you'd rather be where you killed yourself to be but it's

not bad here in row F, you could
have your own sweaty ticket, you could
wear your favorite sleek black clothes
out loud in this public place, you could
let the maestro lead you through the moods,
the survivable moods.

The God Hole

Seventy degrees on the winter solstice,
   a yule moon sifting through ragged clouds
into the undersides of trees
   —lamplit, pearly gray—like the bellies
of huge snails whose branchy horns test

   whatever it is the winter birds
sail in on—or, not birds,
   but the wings we were meant to put on later
that same night—I knew that about us
   then. You had gone into your house

to pack the last things. From the yard,
   I could hear you
sorting out the things that, between us,
   we'd have two of—things you'd give away
or, doubting us, store.

   Our love then was still
a slowly drying idea, pale underneath
   where we had not yet turned it over
to find that it was a traveled shoe
   whose sole-hole eats anything . . .

You opened the door
   and stood there, silhouetted,
the boxes stacked around you like a cardboard shell.
   This, I thought,
is a man from outer space,

from a planet where the slow
crawl of contingency
    wears clear streaks in the filmy air
through which God—telescopic,
    from Its orbits—

can view the slow-moving creatures moving
    along in their sealed world, where some
(asked to leave?)
    move even slower, even dearer, even toward
one another.

II

Our Mutual Friend in Heaven

I remember our trek and talk
in those November fields
where the train went through
not too many hours after our friend D.
chose to die—the leaves
still rouged by rusty whistles
so any truth we uttered caught
in autumn's red, sore throat.

I remember your postman-shoes
left prints too deep for one man
as though your job forced you to carry
some package weighty as heaven
(huge, undeliverable fishbowl
your best friend stuck his head in).

I remember the body our D.
had so recently hinged open: how I
sat down, then, to rest on the small cliffs.
And how, from there, I could see the poplars waver
in their unaccustomed splendor
(they'd been, while D. was here,
the second-most majestic things on earth).

Later, we slept in his abandoned corner room
like two letters dropped in a box,
both of us addressed to that city where D.
must already have been snugged
in his blankets of wind, in his in-
decipherable state, and country, of mind

to which only I had been stamped
with his kisses, in time.

Which must be the reason
you wanted me, wanted
to enter the same body
where D. had rehearsed his deaths—

the sudden sweet gravity of the cock collapsing, after,
back onto the warm salt dune of its own thigh.
I remember how, crying, you opened me

not with the blades of steam
that rose from the lake where we'd sent out
the tardy lifeboat we had made
of matchsticks, matchsticks
(his exquisite boniness, why didn't
we see through it?),

but rather by blind tearing
(was it D., inside the earth?)
the way I'd ripped open your note describing
the way you'd ripped open his note.

I arrived at the red, bad-news hour.
I stayed till you woke me to come
on your early postal rounds
and made me reach my arm
into the damp numbered slots to let drop
what might say *Love*,
but what might begin *Dear John*.

I think, now, you did it to give me
(women require it, too)
my own this-world mystery
to practice entering into.

Etiquette

The man and the woman enter
the bar in that order: male, fe-male, the root
word and its bud. From the way he strains to hold the heavy wood
door for her—his chapped, heroic
arm jutting out from the impossible
fulcrum of his groin where his body will not bend,

(not like the Victorian lady outside who bends
forever, always about to enter
the man-made harbor and leave her impossible
tail still carved into the prow of the boat like a root
marooned and drying in the hot salt air that the hero
rehydrates with kisses in the novel the Victorian lady would

have written in golds on the water's surface, that would
have made tourists bend
over the guardrails to read, our hero
among them, would have made the whole shipload finally enter
the sea to decode the text—the roots
of shifting, womanly surfaces, the possible

layers of meaning in water, and the impossible
cold where the lady's words settle on the bottom among wooden
relics of this and that—if she only had a pen, if she knew the route
to fame—); and from the way the woman, the human woman, bends
beneath the man's arm, her spine like green wood as she enters
the bar, its black wave of noise, divining what she can't quite hear: *oh*'s

and *ah*'s from those of us who glimpse her oh-
so-recently tousled hair and think of the possible
poses in which he tousled it, no doubt entering
his name upon the deepest ledger of her body where it would
count, or so we think she must have told him as she bent
above him saying *now   yes   now* and he dug like a mole for the root

he thought he left in her, and made their small boat rock, nearly uproot
the anchor. On the prow the lady remains a tight-lipped hero.
The boat keeps tossing with their motions and the lady bends
like the stirrer in the drink the man just bought the woman. It's possible
they'll go on like this. Probably the wooden
lady will stay mute. Tomorrow they'll sail on, anchor, do what's called
        love and then enter—

enter what?—a harbor bar? the "world"? with the same heroic
gestures. At each watering place along their watery route, she'll make
        her entrance
through the bend of his wood arm. *See*, their bodies say, *how love's
        nightliness is possible?*

The Saving Grace of Mozart

After the stroke, my grandmother, snug
   in the nautilus of her own curled spine

would slow-stab violent gestures with the one
   knitting needle she clenched on her good side

as she tried to talk—to whom?—
   we knew she couldn't hear our answerings

even if we had been
   there to answer.

We kept her alive, I think,
   by leaving her chiefly alone

—scary, to get visited
   by vaguely familiar giants—,

though once in a fit of benevolence
   we squeezed into her humid room,

the four of us: my sister   me
   the one flute   and the other.

How did we discover silver speech
   would be the thing to reach

her ears' remaining registers?
   As if disability

distills us to a purity
　　where only beauty reaches us

(we knew *we* weren't beautiful,
　　but the flutes, the flutes!).

The rest I guess we generate
　　of our own accord

the way, with the clear side of her bitter brain,
　　she once wove scratchy sweaters

that we still dutifully donned
　　on our quick summer visits.

But this once we stayed, we bobbed,
　　we played accurate Mozart,

the paired flutes shuttling back and forth to scale
　　the damp woof her dying left across the air,

scrambling to reach a high, sturdy dryness
　　they hoped would transport them once and for all

and maybe take her, too,
　　into the realm of the boy-genius

in punctual heaven—.

Grackles

The already-dead quit answering
   and commence to send in grackles, black
floaters at my vision's edge
   between *want* and I *want*.
What has my father tired of

   that makes him want to go there
and be punched out in the v-shape
   a child draws for any
distant bird until the blue sky blooms
   with crowded crayoned crotches?

My father brims with cells.
   Sex is what's undone him
and what, they say, needs carving out.
   It is the biggest grackle.
It struts, it caws, it knows.

   Strutted. Cawed out. Knew.
Now in a white bucket.
   Now swung down to the lab.
Henceforth he is his percentages:
   After blahblah months the chance of blah is blah . . .

Was it the *noise* of birds, the creaking
   kitchen beaks?
What made the winged chair hold him?
   Are birds what made him tired
all the evenings of his life?

And should I change my name? I was willing
to strap on the wings, myself—
     But then this grackle racket,
this sound sun bounces off of,
     this thing he tried to say

and walked off the street into Bellevue
     and asked for a good shrink to say it to
and when she didn't work, another.
     (What voices in the kitchen,
what stew bird in the pot?)

     Holier Father, listen.
Lately he does not rise.
     He wants to take the chair with him
in case there aren't enough,
     he wants

to bring the deep plush wings
     that caught
the head that lost track
     of the body that wanted
to cry like these cries.

On Giving My Father a Book About Roses

Only child, he draws a child
upon a horse within a house upon a
—horse/house/hoarse—globby
thicket of graphite on graphite
piling up into a gawky rose

whose pistil the child lifts
—yellow pencil as thick as a horse's leg—
and draws that child who draws
that child who draws that
drawing child.

If he had had a brother
to remind him to move the pencil.
If he had had a horse, his own
large, large-eyed thing on whom

nothing is lost.
But that is what the rose is.
The rose on page one,
page one of the book
I gave him an hour ago.

Now he concentrates so hard
on this page he doesn't remember having seen
that the rose is a thicket of flesh-petals
breaking the tan soil of his brow.

And this hour spent talking of roses,
the one out in the trunk, concrete half of the gift,
of how we would plant it according to the book
on the sun-bleached side of his new "assisted" dwelling . . .

You can have back this rose,
you big Universe Bud whose shuttlecock-face
probes the dark interplanetary dirt.
You can have back the book, Cosmic Bookstore.

But when you excise this hour from his mind
—and me in that hour, and the small, coherent
splice of talk about roses,
I may not be able to forgive.

His face blooms scarlet,
his chin darts down for shade
as he has to ask my name

the way you have to re-ask the fancy names of roses
not because you weren't listening but because
you don't happen to have a head for roses.

How frightening to find,
an hour later, on your lawn,
—an hour later than *what?*—
the splayed gloves, sharp-edged shovel, the
earth itself in a body-sized bag.

What
was somebody going to plant there
(did he plant me knowing what I was?)

and do I own up to the book about roses
now that the giving
rattles in his brain like an extra star
the ones who're science-smart, or dead,
already know *is* dead?

The drawn rose was always dead.
But it was the one that, pointing to the page,
we had agreed to plant.
I had agreed to plant.

May all the tiny grimbled-up lives
in this diatomaceous earth
shore up our storybook rose.
May its roots hoof out of their burlap sock,
may it raise up its apricot-blaze brain,

and may he remember what it is so he can water it,
or, if he can't,
may the rain remember to rain.

Windy Popples, Late October

Where is the big hammock all this tallness
could lie down in? All I want is rest
from my ravenous need for consoling, from all
the thick bark phone lines pointing to a blue call
more comforting than heaven. There's nothing left
to ask for. A little soreness hangs on deftly
in the highest branches. I, too, could sing soprano
once. I used to be able to hit, you know,
the chilliest leaf-dropping notes. The crowd
crowded to hear: at their expense I bowed,
they *clapped*—but not the way this mess of redness
praises wind by poppling to excess.
I never sang too well. These trees express
just trees. All they're willing to teach me is gladness.

Late Valentine

We went like a parti-colored streamer
sucked by jealous wind
from the straw hat of a girl
on the verge of noticing
she's looked at, we

ribboned along, our hot slow cars
anointing the scars
where the cornfields belonging
to X and to Y are sutured, the better

to get the mail in
(and, oh, the bundles of cards now,
dumped at your mama's farm),
the better to get the grain out,
the better little pigs to market.

We slithered, sad and stately.
We lit up Iowa with overkill headlights.
To noon—or you—we must have looked
like the spine of Xmas itself—all the
soft, nervy places in the air between the cars
blazing in our garish self-pity

as if we could really follow you—coy,
dressed-up, not like the boy
we'd just seen you fly back into,
under the layers of undertaker's rouge.

Still, we felt you in front of us,
napping in the long car under the long lid
(a special import, giant-sized,
everyone but you had waited two days for).
Long-heartedness, yours, led us on.

And leads us, although the days stumble
as if they'd been shot in the knees.

We have not yet buried the days.
And we do not intend
to bury the shirt. There is a way

the whole placket of buttons
came off in the paramedic rip:

We keep on finding stray buttons
like little hearing aids scattered
in the room where you must have called out
as the furniture stiffened.

It will take us a while
to unbutton this dumb sorrow.

We will have to practice,
sometimes on each other,
sometimes on each other's
buttons.

Roland Stone
1951–1986

Slow Movement in G

FOR H.

Like the masseuse who never lifts   her hand
from the fever   only you know
your body has   turned into, like

the body you are giving her,   inch by
deeper inch,   down to the scrawled note
your heart ate like evidence   but that

still sings   a little in the range
we humans will acquire   when we learn the shaggy trust
dogs have always had for the blind,   that sings in

a silent screel out from your molten core
reaching   the left foot that is
the scrambled replica   of the body's whole misery

singing that misery   and then
the right   where the same map taps hushed time
and on up to the left ear   (curled fetus, little

unwitting mirror-self)   cocked just
above the sound   it doesn't hear
since it is deaf like you   deaf

to what you want   which is to play
a note called *H.*   You
liquify   and liquify

your wrist to   draw the bow
and quiver   (stunned spider)
on the suddenly   exterior guts.

"Playing"   it's called but over
whose body   whose
womanly   wooden body whose notes

stop short at G   but who
makes you hum, love, you   hum you
help us bear it   the

healing holohedral Halleluia   Halleloo . . .

Storm Bulletin

Too easy to mention the weather.
To say how I see cities under last night's toppled trees—
    the curled, sexual hair of the matted roots,
  and whatever, wet and blinking, made
the pinhole-pinhole-pinholes there, then fled
    to the overpopulated world of the disappeared.

    The trees lie on their sides on embarrassed elbows
and gaze up at the dwellings they
    karate'd, de-guttered, worse—
  from which I see the old,
piecemeal, by ones, slowly, this morning,
    shakily emerge.

    But our house is ok.
Your absence makes things, well, *concrete:*
    sidewalk slabs jut at a number of skies
  like knocked-up bottom teeth,
and the "power lines," downed, thrash in the leaftrash
    as if they could send those bad leaves back

    to the branches' high memory of rooms.
Where were you when it hit?
    Walls of greenish sideways hail and—
  They say when it sounds like a train
(what train were you on?), a train heading straight
    for the house (this house we dared to want?),

head for the lowest place
(my body was not deep enough,
    so what good, love, could I have done you?).
  Too easy to blame it on the weather.
But what thing here isn't lying, still,
    wind-filled, wishing to be heard?

Aubade

After the sadness of apples in August
   gone secretly soft
inside their gorgeous, high-tech skins,
      after the thumbprints I left on them
            multiplied
in the slanting wall of mirrors above the produce bin,

      after they lay still, languishing,
   looked at
by someone not-quite-you,
      after they were sold to make pies
            not love,
after the orchard grass that still remembered them

      swelled with bees, and the bees grew sick
   of sweetness and even
the queen grew sick of sweetness,
      her new generation suspended in apple
            blossom
honey so that, later, they complained

      the world for them would always be doomed,
   everlastingly
semi-sweet;
      after the fall, our fall
            and the other, after
we'd ripened

in the heat of our one body,
   after
we'd tasted us and said it was good,
    after we realized we could sell
      such a red
as our skins had become by just

    touching roundnesses,
   after, when just looking
across the room at each other
    we could make the air crisp, make
     the sweet places harden,
after we fell into a sleep so smooth even

    our dream blushed as we peered out
   through its rosaceous skin—;
morning
   broke
    the truth back into us,
it split us to the core

   of what we each had been.

Midwestern

Lately, where my body ends, yours begins.
Or so I keep thinking, although you are far.
It's hard to say, sometimes, just what has been.

To reconstruct the feel of it, give me some men
—all strangers, please—to synchronize the bar
stools' twirling: when the one called *me* winds down you begin

to stir the afternoon. A fifth of gin,
too, please, to symbolize how clear we were
each to each. I know just what has been

between us; it still is. My body here, lupine,
hungry to hear you say how far
it is to where this wanting ends and you begin

the drive back over red, real miles again.
Come back: Galesburg, known for trains, Star-
lite Motel where giant neon lips flash *What's Been*

Can Be Again. There's a compass in
your body. My open legs? Your two-point star
that lights up where our one body ends. Or else begins:
beneficent, hard to hold, just what's always been.

Christmas at the Buddhists'

Christmas at the Buddhists'
we always play charades.

Call it a way
of getting through the day
converted souls still flicker at.

Call it a way
of converting into play
the workaday, Top 40 lives they mislaid
somewhere on the path.

They'd call it the way
and stop there: just
the way.

Later, they bow heads and chant
their unison prayer so fast—
sounds like:
a conductor rattling off stations
commuters know.

My lips don't move
though each of my hands is held and held up
with theirs around the candlelight.
And who's to say the weak link
doesn't complete the chain

in the eyes of whatever
our circle of lifted hands
like neatly scalloped waves
practices breaking toward.

I qualify, like them, for admittance
by my emptiness.
I come to my sister's table
to be filled.

French Horn

The name, you might think,
if you're twelve, and you know,
is like those kisses

someone will do to you
if you're lucky and remember
to let him. But how far down

your body will he go?
There's something like entrails
about all this gaggle of tubing

like a hospital i.v.
or how someone in the textbook
jailed up Cleopatra's hair.

And launching out of silence
to hit just the right note
is next to impossible, and so, in this, it is like

kisses, also. In public this thing
should wear a dress over its guts
like the girls who are good at it—one

especially, born
with no right hand.
But you have to put your hand *in*

to mute it, or let it moan . . .
What our bodies
were suited for was an

increasing mystery,
which may be why we envied
her efficient, perfect flipper

that somehow worked best for this
as if the same template of wind
around whose body the brass tubes

had formed, had formed
her body, so she belonged more
to the horn than

the other way around.
We could see it carrying her home from school,
we could see its bell blooming

in her sweet broad face, and of course
it made us jealous, how she retained
1st chair, how the bandleader doted

on her for whom the centuries of hounds
must have bounded,
after which had galloped

the lord's most velvet page
with his second, keyless, exterior, piercing
and definitely most heavenly curled brass throat.

What was he thinking, that one without the gun
whom all the guns charged after?
What was he saying in the back of his mouth

that narrowed and loosened
at will around the source of breath and made
the fall air need him? Was he that much like a woman

he needed one like her
as if to know himself by the slight
mammalian difference of his hand

stroking hers? We imagined
her sleep, where we thought she must have worn it,
(we worried, too, *If I die before I wake* . . .)

her right "hand" still lodged
in that brass extravagance with which
she'd be fit to shake heavenly hands;

and, on the pillow, like a receiver left dangling
in case a wayward god needed someone to confess to,
the trumpet-flower mouthpiece, open-ended

as the story in which a fox gets caught
doubling back to speak his peace
into her oiled body

which curves and flowers and over
the centuries develops three keys, three
left-handed means

that allow us to fast-forward in the one
stunning rip from deformity to grace
that opens, that is

the hunt.

III

Vision Near Ice

I had not known you would return to me like this,
older, and tall, as if time
    does pass in that bigger world—
I had not even hoped.

But what did they do to you?
How did the hungry cells divide and grow
    when the mouth that had opened for kisses and spoons
did not ever arrive, and even the bodily wanting

went extinct?
Doesn't what circumnavigates the seeable
    —like grace, or these skaters
who seem born with their blades on,

circling the soft spot on the pond
like gentle thoughts that circled
    your and my young heads in those first months
when just a membrane divided us from stars—

doesn't whatever it is
want to save itself from time and won't it
    go to any lengths, even—see the skaters?—
won't it carve lovely gashes around the pond's glass eyes

in which the ordinary seasons are otherwise
too glimpsed?
    There are figures, perfect ones, left on the ice.
The perfect parents look on, their twin mufflers

ring their necks.
And all your life you skated toward them, asking
　　the weather to stay cold until you reached them
　　though that made it cold when you arrived in their arms.

All this I knew until
you came back having eaten more than ice
　　and lifted me with real arms, stronger than before
　　—Shall I say "before"?

Before you were invisible?
Before the air's hand
　　slapped down over the hole in the river, before
　　you rose back through, tightening this room?

If I am with you, love,
time is somewhere else and the ice
　　that isn't you seals
　　all rivers against you for good.

The Name of God

You, whose name
   I am trying to learn
late in my life,

is it too much to ask
   the battered roses to teach me?
They keep on waving and waving

their torn sleeves
   like ladies on a dock
though the ship's long gone.

Too much to ask this grass
   darkening in rain
like the hair on my head

that a man
   once called beautiful,
that also darkens as I stand

at this fountain in the rain?
   I have always preferred
the rise and fall of predictable plots,

though this one's marred
   a little, I confess,
by random August rain.

I have wandered quite accidentally
   into the garden.
The angel here is stone—

how beautiful she must have been
    inside the marble block
where only you could see her.

Then money made the sculptor
    chip away her clothes, flick
the last chink

from the shapes called *lips*.
    Did she offer up your name then,
—a cry unplugged from rock—

or did it take the pump
    to lift that word
through the secrets of her body

and spew it out her mouth?
    Ventriloquist, what if
there is no word at all for you

except for water
    that, after I have gone,
will finally carry off

the dummy angel's body?

Maybe the Jay

Maybe the jay resting on the eave right now
is really all mirrors: just a fake blue

stolen from the sky-blue sky.
And the sky's just a blue mote

in Your enormous eye—You,
so big, so pleased with Yourself,

so distantly wondering how we
could subscribe to the theory that sex

makes birds dress up in blue.
How they project themselves into everything,

You think, and shrug, and a tidal wave ensues.
But what have You done different

if we are to believe
"In Its own image, God, the parent, made . . ."

and what about this news
that flies in, airmail, in sync

with the jay? My cousin has tested
positive, it seems. Positive. As if

the virus could cheer you up, as in
"think positive," or the "I'm positive, dear!"

that sends the two-lovers-and-then-some,
kissing, back to bed.

It's as if her anorectic frame that always looked
like a negative has suddenly gathered flesh, and now

she's walking out, backlit, into 3-D,
to borrow our futures. Oh, my cousin

is positive, positive:
more than the zero she believed herself to be;

more than the plus of the cross hairs
through which, in terrible retrospect,

we see her crooked arm, the shared
needle of happiness; more

than the charge of glass rubbed with silk
(her glass thighs, the silk

hood hiding the boy's face from us
so we won't blame him later).

And if we've been deficient
in love up till now,

if we didn't orbit her like
a family of electrons, and follow

those clinical "positive suggestions"
we paid for by the hour,

we admit that, though wise,
we should have been wiser,

nobler, now,
we are not Noblest, but

You are, You are,
You are, You are,

so keep her plus-sign aloft on your radar
until we find one needle

sharp as love's *l*, filled with sufficient belief
to kill the symptoms.

Husbandry

Marsupial, he says, *marsupial!*
holding it up by the terribly naked tail, proud
as if he's invented the word, or, better yet,

become it: all morning long
since he'd found it in the henhouse,
shivering, crouched near the sucked-out egg,

itself no more than egg-sized, really,
but missing, now, its own furred shell—
he'd tucked it in his shirt pocket

where it rode all morning,
bulged and shifted, rested and wrestled
like a small exterior heart.

Thus, he made the morning rounds,
feeding all the bigger, the
penned-in animals.

It was dropped, he figured. *An accident*, he figured.
And hadn't he been dropped, so?
Hadn't he seen a motherness trot off

swinging the many ones she loved better
from her swollen underbelly
like a carillon of sucking bells?

So that now he lived alone,
miles from anyone, but with so many animals
an aerial view would lead God to think

what man lacks so much caring for
that a plethora of gentle beasts
gathered around him to soften his days

so *home* came to mean a thick coat waiting
for him to rub his fingers through
at each and every turn: Old Max

and Young Max, the original dogs,
then Maxes to follow, herding
the dingy, uncountable sheep,

foreground to the dozens of horses, the
dozens of long almost-human jaws
where the words so hard to say

are chewed and chewed
and finally pronounced
in glistening field-fulls.

And all this, a setup
to bait the wilder creatures
who come, like the best lovers,

when we're so consumed
with what we think is happiness
we forget to watch for them;

who come, nonetheless,
to visit us domestics, us
more married animals, to sink,

if they can,
their long teeth like thoughts
into the husbanded eggs

and suck out their rightful place in the grand plan
—egg to egg to egg—by which
we believe we might circumvent

(by the planned brood,
the selling off, the day
to drive the mares to stud)

whatever loneliness
too many or too few
creatures make for.

They come, the uninvited, the wild,
the still-too-young, out of their wild
pockets in the woods, into

the farm, just
visiting—like him, like all
the planned-for creatures—just

visiting the farm, visiting
the planet, the particular pocket
of sun's warmth that nests,

for now, among the other stars
like galaxy's *g*: at home
for the moment

language lasts, then off to another word:
good, as in the boy he'd always been, or
gimme, as in, well, now he's unsure

quite *how* to ask for his opossum back,
since he's lowered it
—his whole cupped hand into my

whole cupped hand into which
its little long-nailed feet (birds', maybe?)
dig, a bit—but he's done

displaying his year's best find.
Done with the show-and-tell he drove to town for.
He snatches, tail-dangles it up like a crazy watch

and we, little pocket of fellow-humans gathered, we
watch as it goes
back into his pocket (too late, now, *not* to picture

its little dimple already forming, too late *not* to think:
pocket in *a pocket* in *a pocket*)
as he drops himself back

into the old paid-off pickup's cabin
that seems to have borne them, and that bears them
safely home.

The Sousaphonist

Who among us hasn't so
desired to be the melody
we strangled ourselves in a boa of song?

The Pit

There was one whole spring I descended,
flutes in hands, into a pit
not yet a metaphor, from which,

gazing up at the soles of dancing feet,
I learned about the ardent world
grown people pay to see.

The famous students' faces
were eerie, bottom-lit—
their cheeks' slack bellows

drank up the sold-out dark
as the curtain pulled back
to reveal their practiced stance.

To the right that meant left or the left
that meant right, they danced, they sang with
new names, new beards,

they peered out into the mothered dark
till the spotlight's white orb
caught in the mitts of their throats.

For them, we vamped and vamped, we
caulked up the cracks forgotten lines fell into,
then gracefully resumed when the frantic found their place.

Consider us your lungs, we said.
Consider us a multi-armed parent always there to catch you.
Consider us: one suave trombone who slides you back to key.

We were so damn good
we dressed in mourning to conceal it,
though our veriform axes glinted

like busy, handless scalpels,
shuttling, digging
away at the ghoulish dark. The time

the pogrom got really out of hand
during closing night
of *Fiddler on the Roof*,

and the real leg that broke happened
to belong to the kid due onstage next
to finish the scene,

the stranded bit-part "fiddler" looked desolate,
winglessly perched
on his false-front roof,

his face ablaze with fake dusk
spewing from the rosy gels
and from his deep distress,

knowing finally what it is to be
the center of attention—enough
of a center for the rest of your life

with your teary-eyed face, the
stupid stringless fiddle,
the crazy rocking and miming, the red lights

branding you like taillights
of the last medic chopper lifting off
as the hot battlefield wind you exhale

licks your own face; while
out there in eternity continues the faint crinkling
of programs in hundreds of hands,

your real name printed there in letters
as obvious as the curtains
the dumb kid named Stew

(you can feel him at the edge of your eye)—Stew
who always tried out but went partless
since all he knew how

to be in this world was Stew the Stew—is still
holding on to, too stunned
to do the brazen thing and yank them without the cue

—so the rope pull hangs, a loose udder in his hands,
and the world hangs, sick, in the sickened light
all crazily rocking and miming for its life

on the roof above the pit when
a two-part magic happens: first, the
trickle of palpable notes

climbing up out of the darkness, past
the lost-in-woods face of the conductor
fanning through the thicket of his score,

just a little emanation from the horsehair and catgut
and maple tucked under the little chinny-chin
of the first chair violin

—a scrawny, bowlegged kid who,
despite much snickering, had towed
the machine-gun-shaped case to and fro

and opened it up of his own accord
and held it beneath his jaw so long
it drew forth a tiny mark there, the skin

blooming beyond its cells
outward from the heart in the direction
of the larger air where, now,

the little tune went,
into the tableau's glow where the saved
fiddler *fiddled*, his mad scraping matched

in a kind of pas de deux in air—
the rough stick rhapsodically scraping, the
five hundred parents believing, as

faster and faster he moved the stick and
faster and faster the bow kept up, playing
not just notes but a pretty, made-up song like, hey,

Louis Armstrong would, or Dean, all-state
jazz trumpet—and it was then
into this upside-down waterfall of sound

from pit to roof, the best boy-actor,
the second genius, *Tevye*, strolled,
perfectly in character,

holding up a finger like a tuning fork
to test this strand of notes,
to see if it would break,

and, when it did not, made it look
like a real wind he was in deep need
of testing, saying *Oh, where is my house, I've*

been out drinking, such
a long night, which way, where
is, oh,

(which is just what his father,
one of the 500, always mumbled
—I'd seen the boozed dad

weaving past our tippy house,
begging the vague wind to push him on home—)
so thoroughly believable

it sounded like the script,
and the whole supporting cast
let out a sigh of relief, of belief

that this boy would soon be representing us
on big stages in the big world
after next week's graduation.

There would *be* graduation,
for by now a crutch, an authentic period piece,
two stump-length boards,

had been fashioned in a **T**
by the talented shop-kids who relished
the life in the bowels behind the wings,

and another young man who soon would be dwindled to death
by the kamikaze biology of this century's
boy-loving plague, but who

at that moment had a mere broken leg,
came stumbling onto the stage
in such convincing pain

it startled even the best actor
who clasped him like a real brother, at which cue
we joined them, belting the farewell

like a siren, like an I-do, as Stew
let the sash cord fly up into the catwalks
and the heavy velvet closed

around that brief pair
standing slightly out of place:
star and star-crossed, embraced.

The Year He Tried Business

That year, flying
was more of a dream than usual.

In the airports, the men
were seen to be eating
the plump white tires
of their happy bagels
as they boarded the planes,

and he was glad as they,
bowing his head as he traversed the pavement
in beneficent winds, bowing
further to be taken aboard
the tiny commuter.

And oh, the grand design of it all—
the little planes filling at dawn in the provinces,
delivering their charges to the mother planes
panting on tarmacs in Nashville, Atlanta.

It was time for him to enter
the world's careening happiness,
time to be part of it, up over it, packed in
with all the cheeky others,
bent-kneed, denuded of anything metal
but the plane itself—the going-ness

of the year, the being-among, the leaving-behind,
the sky phone, little lunches, the newspapers other
eyes had touched, though news no longer mattered,
nor did the trusted pilot, the plausible
safety features, the gladly shared
armrests, the sugar for coffee
doled out in little packets because
sweetness *is* attainable.

The House in the Clearing

Once I woke up thirty paces from everything.
It was a morning in one of my lives.
In one of my other lives

something had hunted me—man, or a certain man.
One of them stepped down into the water and kept walking,
so much did he wish to be surrounded.

Is that all it took? And that he'd been awash in me,
that we'd been one sea creature?
Increasingly, a large animal drifted,

heedless, empty-headed,
on the dirty rim of sight
and it would not go away

or weigh what it weighed.
You weren't that owl,
and you weren't that deer with the broken leg, were you?

Tweedy, my sister said about the owl,
opening her hinged arms in front of her face
like a child miming dinosaur jaws

to show how big he was, settling near her.
But though I sat on my porch
saying *Tweedy Tweedy*, and

owl? owl?, and *you-who-can-look-
behind-you-and-see-the-past*
(I wanted to see it, too—mine, and his—how, for instance,

I came to live in that clearing, that
moat-of-grass across which
nature's Big Things

had to travel naked,
exposing to the cannon-fire of my amazed glance
their bright, ponderous, more-than-human faces),

but all I could see
was the dent where your wingspan
parted the air.

If I had dived through there,
if I had learned to fly,
how would you have received me?

Not, I think, like the doe with the broken leg
who you left alone. I still see
the three punched cloven notes in the snow,

then the one long drawn out one, just
like the opening of Beethoven's Fifth.
So the rest of the symphony

must have been meant to win her back.
These words are meant to win back
my place in the world.

I will go forth now, saying them, saying them,
sometimes like a proud beak in front of my face,
sometimes, a dark muzzle.

Oh wild things, will you hear?

Five O'Clock

FOR S.

Beyond the fence the grass left
uncut for the cows to cut.
But here, such roaring: his arm muscles ripple
as though the earth were upside-down
and he hoisted the mower's bulk overhead,
laboring to unfurl aisles.
He wants me to marry him.
Has been carrying me with those same arms
through all our rooms. Could set me down
in the field. Whatever it is I say.
Hello hello the field always says.
Goodbye goodbye the same green way.
Now I could watch him die or he
could watch me die or could we agree to drive
in one car till a wave washes over the road?
After the cows eat some they keep
chewing and chewing. Eating is better
than being done eating. The swathless field
eats red sun whole, eats shit, eats our mutual air.
We make love, and love. We make supper and supper.
I had not known this want.